.95

Contingency Management

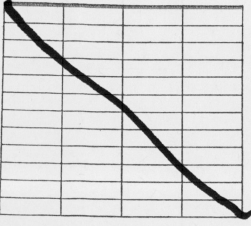
STAFF

KMOR

Special Education
ation
California

ing Company
mpany
io

Published by
Charles E. Merrill Publishing Company
A Bell & Howell Company
Columbus, Ohio 43216

This book was set in Helvetica.
The production editor was Beverly Kolz.

ISBN: 0-675-08708-2

Library of Congress Catalog Card Number: 74-31578

2 3 4 5 6 7 8 9 10 / 80 79 78 77 76

Printed in the United States of America

Contents

Acknowledgments

Special thanks for their contribution in the production of this program go to the following:

> *Richard Denning* and his class at Rowland Avenue School, Covina Valley Unified School District, Covina, California

> *Jerry Hegarty,* Principal
> *Ann Farrow,* Educational Specialist
> *Joseph Perata* and his class
> and
> *Hazel Wiseman* and her class at El Rancho School, Pleasant Valley Elementary School District, Camarillo, California

> *Nancy Lokitch* and her class at Gardner Street School, Los Angeles Unified School District

> *Marilyn Higgins, Charles A. Watts, Bruce Weston,* and *Tim Williams,* Instructional Materials Center for Special Education, University of Southern California

> *Gerald Olson, James Shaw, Dorothy Mortimer,* Washington Elementary Schools, Phoenix, Arizona

James Goff, Media Consultant, Phoenix Productions, San Luis Obispo, California

Bob and Leslie Galeotti, Galeotti Graphics, Long Beach, California

Kathee Prakken, for typing the original manuscript

Introduction

CONTINGENCY MANAGEMENT: A DEFINITION

This program illustrates and describes a very effective technique for motivating students. The method, based on the work of Lloyd Homme, is called Contingency Management, and in simplest terms, it is a contracting system in which the students' successful *task* completion is consistently rewarded by *free time* activity. The students and the teacher actually enter into an agreement. The teacher promises to provide free time for students to engage in self-chosen activities which they enjoy; the students agree to complete a specific amount of academic work in order to "earn" their free time.

Teachers constantly face the challenge of motivating students and of promoting the development of self-management in their pupils. Contingency Management provides some answers for the problems presented by the retarded or slow learner, the student with learning disabilities, the child who is "turned off" to learning, and the student whose behavior patterns inhibit his own learning as well as that of his classmates. The outstanding features of Contingency Management are well-described by Homme (1970) who asserts,

The method can be used at any grade level and with any subject. The method — or variations of it — has been applied successfully with normal children in regular public school classrooms, with children suffering from severe emotional disturbances, by parents within their own families, and in many other situations. As a matter of fact, the successes achieved with behavior management systems of this kind during the past few years have established it as one of the most significant developments of the twentieth century in applied psychology. (Homme, p. ix)

A DESCRIPTION OF THIS PROGRAM

This program is designed to train preservice and inservice teachers in both regular and special education how to implement a Contingency Management system. The complete program consists of this book and four sound-filmstrips:

1. "Contingency Management: Basic Principles"
2. "Contingency Management in the Classroom"
3. "Planning a Contingency Management Program—I"
4. "Planning a Contingency Management Program—II"

All the information needed to implement a Contingency Management system successfully is presented in this book and the filmstrips. The program is self-instructional; it can be used by individuals or with groups. Chapters 1 through 4 of this book provide further exploration of the ideas presented in the accompanying filmstrip through:

1. structured tasks and activities which develop skill in applying the principles of Contingency Management;
2. a short self-test on the filmstrip and text content.

Also included in the book are samples of classroom materials and suggestions for adaptations and further reading on Contingency Management.

The specific ideas and techniques presented in this program have evolved out of several years of experience in training teachers and student teachers in Contingency Management. These training activities were conducted by Bruce Weston and other staff members of the Instructional Materials Center for

Special Education at the University of Southern California and took place in a variety of educational settings from California to Massachusetts. Workshops were held for educators working in hospitals and institutions, special education programs, and regular classrooms as well as for education students at the preservice level. In each instance, the emphasis was on the participants actually implementing (rather than merely learning about) a Contingency Management system with children. Participants were followed and evaluated on their success as contingency managers. Each training experience provided valuable information which led to revisions and refinements in the training content and presentation format. The present program represents the best and most effective elements of all the face-to-face training sessions. Special credit goes to Bruce Weston, Tim Williams, and the core of teachers they helped to train as Contingency Managers who are now trainers in their own right.

HOW TO USE THIS PROGRAM

After viewing each sound-filmstrip and completing the self-tests and tasks in each chapter, the learner will be able to:

1. Identify the major principles of Contingency Management with at least eighty percent accuracy (Filmstrip 1; Chapter 1).

2. Plan each step necessary in setting up a Contingency Management system in the classroom. Criterion: one hundred percent accuracy on tasks presented in this book (Filmstrips 2, 3, 4; Chapters 2, 3, 4).

3. Implement a Contingency Management system. To be considered successful, the system designed by the learner will include *all* of the following observable characteristics:

   a. The classroom (or a section of the room) divided into a *task area* (where students work on academic tasks and assignments), and an *RE* area (where children go after task completion to engage in *self-chosen* reward activities).
   b. A visible *RE menu* or list of activities from which students can choose for their free time (RE time).
   c. Nonverbal signal(s) which (1) individual students can use to indicate need for teacher attention and (2) the teacher

uses to signify the time for students to return to task area.

d. The school day (or a portion of it) is scheduled into a series of *cycles*; each cycle has two parts — a *task* time and a *reward* time. Upon completion of assigned task, student is excused to RE area.

In order to meet the above objectives, it is suggested that learners follow the Skill Sequence Checklist below. Each phase or step in the program is important, as is their sequence.

SKILL SEQUENCE CHECKLIST

Learning Phase I   _____   1. Read Introduction

_____   2. View Filmstrip 1

_____   3. Read Chapter 1

_____   4. Complete Task I

_____   5. Take Self-Test

Learning Phase II   _____   1. View Filmstrip 2

_____   2. Read Chapter 2

_____   3. Take Self-Test

Learning Phase III   _____   1. View Filmstrip 3

_____   2. Read Chapter 3

_____   3. Complete Tasks IV, V

_____   4. Complete Activity I-A *with* students

_____   5. Complete Activity I-B, Tasks VI and VII

_____   6. Take Self-Test

Learning Phase IV   _____   1. View Filmstrip 4

_____   2. Read Chapter 4

_____   3. Complete Activity II

Learning Phase IV cont'd.	_____	4. Complete Activities III or IV
	_____	5. Complete Activity V
	_____	6. Take Self-Test

From this point on, you will be implementing the Contingency Management Program with students.

Learning Phase V	_____	1. Read Chapter 5, pages 67 to 69
	_____	2. Complete Task X
Covers	_____	3. Implement Contingency Management System Program Day 1
one		
week's	_____	4. Read pages 74 to 76 Chapter 5
time		
	_____	1. Implement CM System Program Day 2
	_____	2. Read pages 77 to 79 Chapter 5
	_____	1. Implement CM System Program Day 3
	_____	2. Read pages 80 to 81 Chapter 5
	_____	1. Implement CM System Program Day 4
	_____	2. Read page 82 Chapter 5
	_____	1. Implement CM System Program Day 5
	_____	2. Read pages 83 to 84 Chapter 5
	_____	3. Complete Task XI

SKILL SEQUENCE CHECKLIST (Continued)

Learning Phase VI   _____   1. Read Chapter 6

    Covers one   _____   2. Complete Task XII
    week's time   _____   3. Implement CM System
                                       for second week

Contingency Management: Basic Principles

Before beginning this chapter, view the sound-filmstrip labeled "1, Contingency Management: Basic Principles."

The main ideas from the filmstrip are further explained in this chapter. When you have viewed the filmstrip and completed the activities in this chapter, turn to the self-test on page 15 and check your progress.

How to manage children in the classroom is a major concern of today's teachers; lack of ability in classroom management is a major reason for teacher failure. The success or failure of an instructional program depends on the teacher's ability to establish and maintain a classroom environment that is conducive to learning. (Hankins 1973, p. 84)

In filmstrip 1 you learned the definition of high probability behaviors and how these can be used to reward or reinforce low probability behaviors. When high probability behaviors (HPBs) are used to strengthen low probability behaviors (LPBs) in the classroom situation, we call the HPBs by another name which is easier to explain to students. HPBs, then, are also called REs or *reinforcing events* because they refer to activities and materials which students *choose* themselves and which are rewarding to them. In the next filmstrip you will see how the teacher makes such activities and materials available to students in a specific area of the classroom designated as the *RE area.*

Before you decide to implement a Contingency Management program in a classroom, you are urged to consider some philosophical or ethical issues:

1. *Reinforcement:*

   A major part of becoming an adult is learning to interact successfully with the people, objects, and events in one's environment. Each interaction contributes either positively or negatively to the process of becoming an effective and self-fulfilled individual. As educators we have the responsibility of arranging environmental events for the learner. Teachers assign tasks, grade papers, smile, scold, ignore, and hug; each of these actions is an "environmental event" which can influence, or even control, the behavioral responses of students. In other words, teachers by their every action reinforce both positive and negative behaviors in children.

   The issue of freedom and control is frequently presented as an argument — a powerful one — against the application of reinforcement principles. This argument overlooks the simple but inescapable fact that the behavioral principles which serve to inhibit or enhance learning operate anyway regardless of whether we choose to recognize them. All behavior has a consequence or a result. We learn to behave in a certain way to obtain a desired consequence or reward. Receiving the consequence or reward is therefore *contingent* on the performance of specific behaviors. Haring and Philips (1972) point out that

We occupy our homes contingent on rent or mortgage and tax payments. Our salaries are contingent on job performance . . . the contingencies of our environment, then, control our behavior and can predictably influence our response. (p. 12)

Contingency Management is simply a *fair*, *consistent*, and *systematic* way of insuring that students receive meaningful rewards for their efforts to behave in socially and academically acceptable ways. "It involves a statement of the functional relationship between the child's responses and their consequences — that is, a statement of what type and frequency of reinforcement will follow a particular response" (Haring and Phillips 1972, p. 13).

Some teachers believe that students should behave in acceptable ways all the time, and that when they do they are merely doing "what they're supposed to do," and do not need to be rewarded. Such a point of view overlooks a significant fact about human behavior; it is the fact that rewards strengthen the behavior they follow. The use of rewards for work accomplished, or behavior displayed by the student, can increase the student's rate and level of acceptable responses. The goal of a Contingency Management system is to arrange the classroom conditions in such a way that students learn to manage their own contingencies effectively.

2. *Bribery:*

A Contingency Management system is *not* bribery. When someone is *bribed*, he typically receives a reward or pay-off for doing something he would not do otherwise. Usually a bribe is used to persuade a person to engage in a behavior which is in some way illegal or unethical. These characteristics are not present in a Contingency Management system.

3. *Positive Approach:*

Contingency Management is a *positive method* of changing behavior. Punishment does not have a place in this system. While punishment obviously can bring about at least short-term changes in behavior, its use produces unwanted side effects. Often all the child learns through punishment is to avoid getting caught the next time. In addition, the child may develop negative feelings toward the punisher. Reluctance to eliminate punishment as a classroom management technique often stems from a concern as to whether it is realistic for a child to exist in a more or less totally positive environment. Williams and Anandam (1973) have a good answer:

The child who is most likely to experience positive reinforcement outside the classroom is the child who has experienced positive reinforcement in the classroom. If positive reinforcement is the most effective procedure to use in teaching academic skills and building self respect, it should also maximize the child's likelihood of success outside the classroom. (p. 29)

Task I

In order to experience personally how Contingency Management works, complete the following exercise:

1. Take a few minutes to think about how you feel: What are some things you really like to do? List your high probability behaviors here:

   _____

   _____

   _____

   _____

2. Now, what are some things that are difficult for you to do or things you don't like to do but should do? List your low probability behaviors here:

   _____

   _____

   _____

   _____

3. What behaviors from list 1 would you pair with specific behaviors in list 2 in order to increase the probability that you will accomplish some of those things you don't really enjoy doing?

LPB	HPB
First I will:	Then:
_____	_____
_____	_____
_____	_____

Now compare your responses with those on the next page.

Answer Sheet—Task I

1. Some possible HPBs might be:
    drinking coffee, coke, beer
    watching television
    jogging
    making a cake
    eating
    listening to music
    relaxing
    your favorite fantasy
    washing your hair
    talking on the telephone
    etc., etc., etc.

    The behaviors *you* listed on the previous page are REs for you. After you complete each section in this training program, select one of the REs from your list as your reward. In the event that you find working through this program rewarding in and of itself, you may add this activity to your list of HPBs!

2. Some possible LPBs might be:
    washing dishes
    reading a book
    mowing the lawn
    studying
    saving money

    The behaviors *you* listed on the previous page are LPBs for you.

3. If you work out a Contingency Contract for yourself from your lists of HPBs and LPBs, it might look like this:
    First I will study   Then eat
    First I will wash dishes   Then watch TV
    First I will eat my peas   Then eat my dessert
    (Homme 1970, calls this Grandma's Law.)

Task II

*Self-Test on Basic Principles
of Contingency Management*

Directions: In the following questions, mark *all* the alternatives
which you think are correct.

1. Contingency Management is basically a contracting system.
   The contract should specify:
   a. an amount of time
   b. an amount of work
   c. a certain task
   d. a choice of tasks

2. Every contract has two parts: the task and the reward. The
   contract should:
   a. be acceptable to both the teacher and the student
   b. insure that the student does a lot of work
   c. enable the teacher to choose the reward
   d. provide a reward appropriate to the task

3. At first, the teacher should accept:
   a. only perfect performance
   b. successful attempts to complete the task
   c. approximations

4. In order for the contract system to be effective, the reward
   must be contingent on task behavior. This means that:
   a. the reward is given after performance
   b. the reward is given as an incentive
   c. receiving a reward depends on passage of time

5. Given any two behaviors, one will be preferred over the
   other. The *preferred* behavior is called:
   a. the LPB
   b. the HPB
   c. an RE

6. In a Contingency Management system, LPBs are:
   a. low probability behaviors
   b. behaviors which the student enjoys
   c. behaviors which occur infrequently
   d. behaviors the teacher wants to eliminate

7. The occurrence of the less preferred behavior can be increased most effectively if:
   a. the student is punished for not completing tasks
   b. getting to engage in an HPB is made contingent on performing the LPB
   c. the teacher praises the student

Check your answers with those on the following page.

Answer Sheet—Task II

1. b. an amount of work
   c. a certain task

2. a. be acceptable to both the teacher and the student
   d. provide a reward appropriate to the task

3. b. successful attempts to complete the task
   c. approximations

4. a. the reward is given after performance

5. b. the HPB
   c. an RE

6. a. low probability behaviors
   c. behaviors which occur infrequently

7. b. getting to engage in an HPB is made contingent on performing the LPB

Contingency Management in the Classroom

Before beginning this chapter, view the sound-filmstrip labeled "2, Contingency Management in the Classroom." The main ideas from the filmstrip are further explained in this chapter. When you have viewed the filmstrip and read the text of this chapter, turn to the self-test on page 24 and check your progress.

If the teacher views the classroom as an environment within which the child acts, and if he uses his knowledge concerning principles of behavior to arrange the events in that environment, he can modify the child's behavior in a predictable direction. (Haring and Phillips 1972, p. xi)

Filmstrip 2 gave you a brief glimpse into a classroom where a Contingency Management program was in operation. This experience may have generated more questions about Contingency Management than it answered. Before dealing with the specific steps involved in implementing such a program, we would like to discuss some of the questions typically raised by teachers and student teachers.

1. *What constitutes a "contract"?*

   A contract is a statement of contingencies which are acceptable to both the teacher and the student.

In his book on contingency contracting, Homme (1970) has stated ten general rules of contracting. We have already covered some of the rules up to this point. Two important rules for a successful contract which we have not yet dealt with are that the terms of the contract must be *clear* and that the contract must be *positive.*

A *clearly* stated contract says, "Answer five math problems, then have five minutes in the RE Center." "The child must always know *how much* performance is expected of him and *what he can expect as a payoff"* (Homme p. 20).

Homme emphasizes that the contract must be stated *positively.* A contract saying, "I will not keep you in at recess if you do these math problems," is not positive.

Both sides of the contract (task and reward) must be positive. "If you don't get out of your seat, you may have five minutes in the RE area" is not positive on the task side. On the other side, "biting nails" may be an HPB for a student but most would agree that this activity would be an unacceptable RE.

We suggest that you read Dr. Homme's book for further explanation of the rules for Contingency Contracting.

The method of contracting demonstrated in the filmstrips and discussed in this book differs in some ways from other methods of contingency contracting you may have used or read about. The approach described here involves contracting for a series of short individual assignments or tasks. Rewards are frequent and immediate. General terms and conditions of the contracting agreement are discussed verbally with the individual student or class. Specific contract conditions are written for each individual child on a daily schedule.

The series of tasks scheduled for each student is interspersed with an appropriate amount of time for defined RE activities.

There are many variations of this approach in use, such as contracting for completion of an entire unit of study, written contracts for a course grade (high school and college classes), and student-controlled contracts. Some of these variations will be described more fully in chapter 6.

The distinction that we are making is that Contingency Management is a *total* management system designed to be used with a whole class or with selected students for their entire school day.

2. *How does Contingency Management allow for individual student development?*

Several authors in discussing contingency contracting address this issue.

The contract method makes possible a relatively simple and easy method of individualizing instruction. Each student can enter into contracts which fall within his ability range and are congruent with his interest patterns and learning style. The goals of learning are clear so that each student knows precisely what is expected of him. (Hankins 1973, p. 286)

An effective contract provides a number of different options to students. Students under the same contractual arrangement might be pursuing very different activities. Nevertheless, each student has essentially the same rights and privileges as any other student. (Williams and Anandam 1973, p. 31)

It teaches them responsibility for their work, as well as something about contracts, that will affect their future lives. It also makes them more aware of their abilities, since they must make judgments about themselves with this system. (Glavin 1974, p. 84)

Although we are presenting a management system for an entire class, this does not mean that every student is doing the same thing for the same amount of time. Not only are students involved in different RE activities, but they are involved in those activities for varying amounts of time depending on how long it takes them to complete their individual task assignment.

3. *What physical arrangements are necessary in the classroom?*

In filmstrip 2 you saw a classroom that was physically divided into two distinct areas — a task area and an RE area. The necessity to divide the room into separate areas depends largely on the needs of the students. If you have students who need a great deal of structure and take their cues from their physical environment, distinct boundaries for areas are desirable and perhaps necessary. If you are operating an open classroom and using contingency management, your activity or learning centers may be used simultaneously by students for task assignments and RE activities.

4. *Why post an RE menu?*

A posted RE menu makes public what activities are available, allowable and agreed upon. The child is not unaware of what is being done to change or modify his behavior.

Williams and Anandam (1973) are convinced

that teachers should spend considerable time helping children to become aware of the contingencies controlling their own behavior and to identify modes of behavior which would produce more positively reinforcing consequences. (p. 22)

Task III

*Self-Test on Contingency Management
in the Classroom*

Directions: In the following questions, mark *all* the alternatives which you think are correct.

1. Which of the following are examples of clear and positive contracts?
   a. If you get your homework right, I will have a nice surprise for you.
   b. If you aren't on time for class, you won't get to see the movie.
   c. When you finish your cleanup activities, you can play with the rabbits for five minutes.
   d. Read pages 50-56 of your text and take the progress test.
   e. Complete the ten problems on pages 20-24; check your answers. Take a minute of free time for each correct answer.

2. Some advantages of the Contingency Contracting system are that it:
   a. makes it easy for the teacher because all students are doing the same thing
   b. allows for individualization of instruction
   c. teaches students to be responsible for their work
   d. facilitates student-teacher interaction

3. When operating a Contingency Management system, the classroom:
   a. must be very structured
   b. can be open and flexible
   c. might be divided into two distinct areas
   d. should contain a variety of options for RE time
   e. may be structured according to the needs of the class

4. An RE menu is:
   a. a list of activities to choose from
   b. a choice of food available for snack time
   c. posted in the classroom

Check your answers with those on the following page.

Answer Sheet—Task III

1. a. Incorrect because reward is not clearly stated.
   b. Incorrect because it is stated negatively.
   c. Correct.
   d. Incorrect because it does not specify a reward.
   e. Correct.

2. b. allows for individualization of instruction
   c. teaches students to be responsible for their work
   d. facilitates student-teacher interaction

3. b. can be open and flexible
   c. might be divided into two distinct areas
   d. should contain a variety of options for RE time
   e. may be structured according to the needs of the class

4. a. a list of activities to choose from
   c. posted in the classroom

3

Planning a Contingency Management Program – I

Before beginning this chapter, view the sound-filmstrip labeled "3, Planning a Contingency Management Program — I." The main ideas from the filmstrip are further explained in this chapter. When you have viewed the filmstrip and read the text of this chapter, turn to the self-test on page 45 and check your progress.

Having selected the appropriate contingencies for the planned procedure, the next step is to find an *environment* that is suitable for the program of behavior change; an environment where the desired behavior is most likely to occur and where incompatible behaviors are least likely to occur.... The environment must be arranged so that it is *possible to control the contingencies.* (Sulzer and Mayer 1972, p. 11)

THE REINFORCEMENT MENU

In filmstrip 3 you learned that the first step in planning a Contingency Management program is to set up a reinforcement menu. The menu is a list of reward activities (high probability behaviors) from which students may choose. Remember, RE activities are available to the student only upon completion of a specified task (low probability behavior). When a student completes a language assignment, a math assignment, a reading assignment, he is allowed to spend some time doing something he likes.

Before looking at the reward side of the contract in more detail, think about some student behaviors which are *low* probability and which you, as a teacher, would like to increase. Some behaviors frequently mentioned by teachers as being low probability for certain students are:

> finishing work
> following instructions
> taking turns
> talking softly.

Low probability behaviors can be either academic, subject-matter-oriented, or social. Now take a few moments to complete the following two tasks.

Task IV

Think of students you have worked with. List some low probability behaviors which you, as their teacher, would like to see increased.

1. _____

2. _____

3. _____

4. _____

5. _____

6. _____

7. _____

8. _____

9. _____

10. _____

Answer Sheet—Task IV

Some LPBs you might have listed for students are:
asking for more work assignments
making an oral report
researching a problem in the library
solving math problems
writing name
counting to ten
recognizing alphabet letters
spelling correctly
using the dictionary
participating in P.E. activities
keeping quiet while teacher is giving directions
coming to school
making complete sentences with spelling words
memorizing a Spanish vocabulary list
bringing in homework
sitting quietly
asking for homework
doing a science experiment
beginning tasks at appropriate time
coming to classroom on time
staying in seat when requested
asking for help when needed
writing a story
cleaning up
listening when someone is speaking
moving quietly and/or purposefully to Learning Centers

Task V

You have just listed some behaviors which relate to the *task* side of the contract. Now, consider the *reward* side. High probability behaviors can be used to reward low probability behaviors. HPBs are behaviors which the individual enjoys and which he frequently chooses when given the opportunity (e.g., one student might like to look out the window; another student might choose to read a book). Think about the same students as in Task IV.

List some high probability behaviors (HPBs) for those students which are permissible in a school setting and which could be used to reinforce a *lower* probability behavior.

check

1. _____ _____
2. _____ _____
3. _____ _____
4. _____ _____
5. _____ _____
6. _____ _____

In the list above, check those HPBs which will need special equipment or supplies.

Answer Sheet—Task V

Some HPBs you might have listed for students are:

watching films

talking with friend

first in line

painting

puzzles

passing out lunch tickets

feeding fish

punching bag

carpentry

writing letters or notes

typing

looking out window

using scissors

playing ball

combing hair

building blocks

watching TV

playing auto harp

tutoring another student

sitting next to a friend

doing homework for other
classes

drawing pictures

looking at magazines

taking apart equipment (old
radio, etc.)

writing on blackboard

making tapes

being out of seat

building a model airplane

going to the library

Some teachers have found that listening to records and dancing are often chosen as REs by young children. Headsets can be made available so that students can listen to music individually without disturbing others. The tape recorder, listening games, and story records are also good activities. Balance beams and twist boards are inexpensive and fun. Hammers, nails, and scraps of wood are fun for both boys and girls.

Manipulative games and toys such as Legos, Lincoln Logs, erector sets, and building blocks are reinforcing to many students. Typewriters are appealing to all ages; writing on the blackboard is a good reward for younger children. Bean bags to toss and catch and cushions or carpet squares for sitting on while reading a book or looking at a magazine are always popular.

For older students the following suggestions may be helpful:

    models (cars, airplanes)

    record player and headsets for listening to records the students bring from home

    a corner where students can go and just talk

    chess, checkers

    high interest magazines such as *Hotrod*, *Seventeen*, etc.

    running errands for the teacher (notes to the office, nurse, etc.)

    operating A-V equipment

There are many reinforcing activities that require minimal or no special equipment:

> making bulletin boards
>
> writing on blackboard
>
> talking
>
> correcting other students' papers
>
> helping the teacher as an aide
>
> jacks

It is not necessary for the teacher to buy special material and trinkets in order for the program to be successful. Students can bring games and toys from home. The teacher can arrange to exchange classroom materials and equipment with another teacher.

Before continuing with this program, complete the following activity with some students. If you are a teacher, work with your own class; if not, arrange to talk to some students — any age, any grade! Continued work with the same students will be necessary for the remainder of this program.

Activity I–Part A

This activity is to be completed *with students.*

1. Talk with the students about activities they like best. Ask each student what he or she would most like to do for fun at school (HPBs).

If they are slow to offer suggestions, mention an activity you have previously observed students doing with enjoyment, and ask them if they would like to put this on the list.

Occasionally, it might be necessary to remind the students that the activities chosen must be appropriate in the school environment.

2. Make a list, on the blackboard or on a piece of tagboard, of the activities suggested by the students.

Now go to Activity I–Part B.

Activity I–Part B

3. In the space below, copy the list you and the students have made.

NEEDED MATERIALS AND EQUIPMENT

HPBs suggested by students	Already in classroom	Student bringing in	Have arranged to get
1.			
2.			
3.			
4.			
5.			
6.			
7.			
8.			
9.			
10.			
11.			

12.			
13.			
14.			

4. After you and the students have agreed upon the list of RE activities (remember a Contingency Management program must meet the students' needs *and* yours), ask them if they can bring some of the needed materials from home. Check the appropriate space beside each activity listed above.

5. *Just for fun*, turn back to Task V in this chapter and compare with the list you made.

How many items match?   0–5 _____   5–10 _____   10–15 _____

Task VI

The activity list you made is a beginning RE menu. Now, take your list of High Probability Behaviors and design an attractive RE menu. It may be helpful to set it up by categories or areas such as: Games, Art Area, Outdoor Activities.

RE MENU

Answer Sheet—Task VI

This is an example of a menu for younger students. For non-readers, symbols and pictures can be substituted for the words.

FREE TIME ACTIVITIES
"DO YOUR OWN THING"

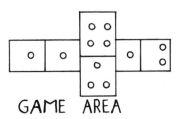

GAME AREA

GAME AREA

Hot wheels	Dominoes
Checkers	Puzzles
Cards	Spill and Spell
Chess	

LISTENING & VIEWING

LISTENING-VIEWING AREA

Records with earphones
Comic books
Cassette recording
Filmstrip viewer

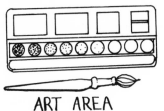

ART AREA

ART AREA

Clay
Models
Coloring
Cut and paste

DOING AREA

DOING AREA

Bouncing ball	Sitting (doing nothing)
Jump rope	Talking
Jacks	Typing
Writing on blackboard	

This is an example of a menu which is appropriate for older students.

GAMES

GAMES

Game of States
Chess
Chinese checkers
Cards
Crossword puzzles

ACTIVITIES

ACTIVITIES

Golf putting
Typing
Weaving
Macramé
Models
Knitting

ENTERTAINMENT

ENTERTAINMENT

Records
Radio
Just reading
Magazines
Just talking

MISCELLANEOUS

MISCELLANEOUS

Resting
Doing homework
Going to library
Using a calculator
Writing letters

ARRANGING THE CLASSROOM

The second step in planning a Contingency Management program is to arrange the classroom. When beginning to implement
the system, it may be helpful to divide the room into two areas
— a task area where students can work quietly on written academic assignments and an RE area where students spend free
time.

Some teachers use a partition (large screen or bookcases) to
divide the room physically. In the task area, all students have
a desk or place at a table where they can work independently
on tasks. There may be tables at the edge or back of the task
area where group activities such as discussions, reading groups,
lesson presentation, demonstrations, may be conducted.

Individual partitions or cubicles may also be used in the task
area. Physical dividers of this kind are not essential, and their
use depends on the particular group of students using the room.

The reinforcement area is used for RE time only. Students are
not permitted to use this area until they have completed their
tasks. All the materials and equipment needed for RE activities
are available in this part of the room. Later on, when students
have learned the system, the room arrangement may become
more flexible.

The following sample room plans may give you some ideas for
arranging your classroom. If your room is small, you might want

to consider an arrangement similar to *Plan A.* In this plan, the tables are grouped together and the RE activities are all located on one side of the room. The A-V equipment to be used as REs is situated close enough to the task area to make it convenient for the teacher to use the equipment for group tasks and presentations. Plan A is a highly structured arrangement.

Plan B represents a classroom which also has two very distinct areas. This room was designed for a special education class and includes student cubicles in the task area. It probably requires more space than the other plans.

The most flexible room plan shown is *Plan C;* it was arranged for a class of thirty-three students and designed for a more open classroom environment. Areas can easily be changed and students quickly regrouped as necessary.

PLAN A

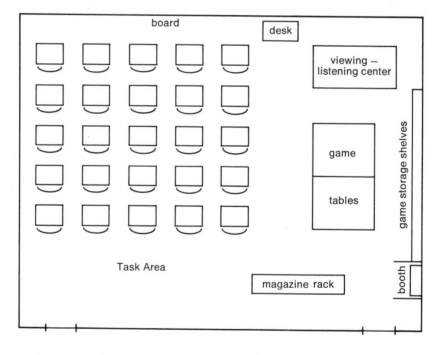

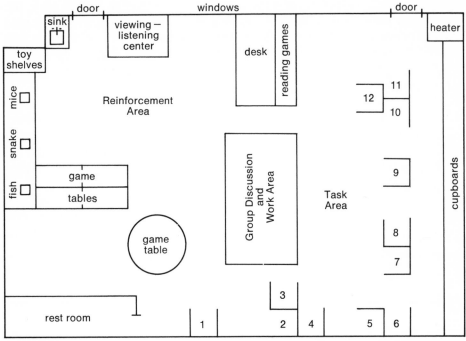

door   windows   door

sink

viewing —
listening
center

desk   reading games

heater

toy
shelves

mice

Reinforcement
Area

12   11

10

snake

fish

game

tables

Group Discussion and Work Area

9

Task
Area

8

game
table

7

rest room

3

1   2   4   5   6

1–12 = student desks

Room Plan contributed by Sue Ogg

PLAN B ↑   ↓**PLAN C**

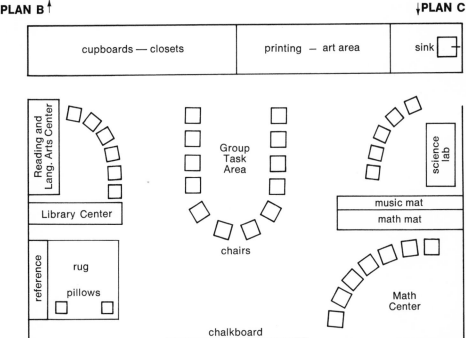

cupboards — closets   printing — art area   sink

Reading and Lang. Arts Center

Group
Task
Area

science
lab

Library Center

music mat

math mat

reference

rug

pillows

chairs

Math
Center

chalkboard

Task VII

Diagram the way you would arrange a classroom into a work (task) area and an RE area.

Task VIII

Self-Test on Planning a Contingency
Management Program—I

Directions: In the following questions, mark *all* the alternatives
   which you think are correct.

1. List the first two steps in implementing a Contingency Management program:

   a. _____

   b. _____

2. In a Contingency Management program, RE activities:
   a. are the same for all students
   b. can be listed on a menu
   c. are the same as HPBs
   d. change from time to time
   e. should be acceptable to both the teacher and the students

3. REs listed on a menu are things that are:
   a. already available in the school
   b. approved by Parents' Magazine
   c. brought in by the students
   d. borrowed from another teacher

4. A typical Contingency Management classroom has areas for

   _____ activities and _____

   _____ activities.

Check your answers with those on the following page.

Answer Sheet—Task VIII

1. a. make an RE menu
   b. plan your classroom arrangement (two areas)

2. b. can be listed on a menu
   c. are the same as HPBs
   d. change from time to time
   e. should be acceptable to both the teacher and the students

3. a. already available in the school
   c. brought in by the students
   d. borrowed from another teacher

4. task activities and reward activities

Planning a Contingency Management Program – II

Before beginning this chapter, view the sound-filmstrip labeled "4, Planning a Contingency Management Program — II." The main ideas from the filmstrip are further explained in this chapter. When you have viewed the filmstrip and read the text of this chapter, turn to the self-test on page 64 and check your progress.

The structure of contingency contracting involves the learner in selecting his own goals, determining ways to reach those goals and choosing reinforcing events. (Jackie Damaske, a successful teacher and Contingency Manager, 1972)

SCHEDULING TASK AND RE TIME

Most teachers are accustomed to organizing the school day around blocks of time devoted to reading, math, etc. Developing a daily schedule for a Contingency Management program is based on the same principle; the difference is that initially the time blocks devoted to each subject area are shortened. The school day is divided into a series of twenty-minute cycles.

Within each cycle, the students complete a task and select an RE. The amount of RE time is what remains of the twenty-minute cycle after the student finishes a task. (At first, this should be about ten minutes.)

A Contingency Management program is most successful when the schedule is designed so that all students in the class start tasks at the same time. The students should be able to finish their tasks within two to three minutes of each other. As soon as a student finishes his or her work, he or she signals for the teacher to come and check it, and is immediately excused to the RE area. Students who finish work quickly get extra RE time.

Teachers find that if a student is not working rapidly, or he is wasting his time in the task area, he will quickly finish up his task when he notices other children being released to the RE area. The influence of the peer group is a powerful motivator. Failure to complete tasks seldom occurs in this system; when it does, the student would remain in the task area while his classmates enjoy RE time. When the rest of the class comes back to the task area, this student begins on a new task also. The only exception to this is when the task is clearly too difficult for a particular student. In that case, it should be modified immediately to fall within that child's ability range.

With older and more mature students, it is possible to increase the task time beyond the suggested ten minutes. Experienced

Contingency Managers have found, however, that the system operates optimally when RE time is kept to five to eight minute periods. This seems to allow sufficient time for the students to be fully reinforced and ready to return to the task area. The teacher should circulate among the students during task time, encouraging them and helping them with their work. This increases their attention span and helps them to remain task-oriented.

The schedule should remain approximately the same for each day during the first week of the program.

HOW THE SCHEDULE WORKS

Two types of signals are required to get the system operating:

1. A *desk signal* used by the student to indicate task completion;

2. A *teacher signal* to call the students back to the task area from the RE area.

Desk Signals

Students remain in their seats in the task area until they are excused by the teacher. This procedure keeps unnecessary talking and moving about to a minimum. The only way that the

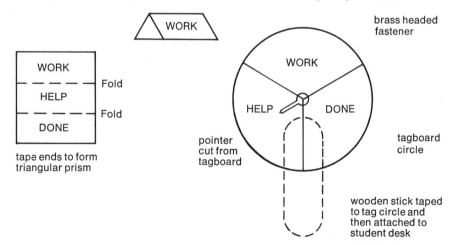

FIGURE 1. Samples of Desk Signals

student can get the teacher's attention is by using a desk signal. Samples of student signals to indicate task progress are shown in figure 1. In both examples, WORK indicates the student is working; HELP indicates the student needs assistance; and DONE indicates the assignment is completed and ready for checking. Color codes are used for each section of the signal (e.g., red for DONE, etc.).

These signals are turned toward the student while he is performing his task, thus emphasizing the concepts of Work, Help, and Done. The teacher working from the back of the area can see at a glance the status of each child. These ideas for student signals were contributed by Mrs. Ruth Kass, a teacher in Scottsdale, Arizona.

The nonverbal desk signal is important because, after turning his signal to "help," a student is free to go on working on another part of his task. Handraising to ask for help immobilizes the student and increases the likelihood of disruptive behavior —the next step may be getting out of his seat, etc. The most successful way to discourage "'talking out" behavior is for the teacher to *ignore* it, and to recognize quickly the student who behaves appropriately. If a child has had difficulty learning the rule about the use of signals, the teacher should reward him immediately by excusing him to the RE area when he displays the correct response for requesting teacher attention.

Students are dismissed to the RE area under the following conditions:

1. Task has been completed successfully or student has made an acceptable attempt.

2. Student's work has been checked off by the teacher or aide; *it is not necessary for the teacher to correct the whole page at this time — a spot check is sufficient.*

Teacher Signals

The use of some *nonverbal signal* (bell, lights, notes on the piano) to call the students back to the task area is a convenient and effective management technique. Thus, all students return from the RE area at the same time. The signal should be used consistently. A nonverbal signal is more effective than verbal directions because it leaves the teacher outside the system. The signal itself becomes responsible for calling the students back from RE time—the teacher is not the "ogre." It also eliminates the tendency to give a verbal command over and over and over again, becoming louder each time.

Students must learn to return quickly and quietly to the task area, and to wait for the teacher's instructions. At first it is a good technique to reinforce "returning to seat" behavior *as soon as* it occurs by immediately sending the students back to the RE area for a few more minutes of free time. Returning to their seats appropriately would be a "task" in this instance.

The teacher should explain to the class that as soon as the signal for return to the task area is given, they are to stop whatever activity they are doing in the RE area and walk quietly back to the task area. Pushing, running, and excessive noise should not be tolerated.

DEVELOPING A FIRST DAY SCHEDULE

On the day that you implement the Contingency Management system with your students, the first task, or series of tasks, involves "introducing and teaching the system" to the students. With handicapped students or young children, you might spend the whole first day doing this.* With older children, one or two cycles may be enough.

Here is a sample of a first day schedule. This schedule remains the same for the first week of program implementation; the tasks change daily.

SAMPLE OF FIRST DAY SCHEDULE

Time	Activity
9:00– 9:20	Task: Introducing the system (Listening)/ RE: Reinforcing event (Unstructured)
9:20– 9:40	Task: Teaching the system: An extremely easy paper and pencil task/RE
9:40–10:00	Task: Teaching the system (cont.): Another extremely easy task/RE
10:00–10:20	Task: Returning to seat after RE/RE: Immediate dismissal to another RE time for returning to seat
10:20–10:35	Task: Recess behavior (lavatory)/RE
10:35–10:55	Task: Phonics worksheet/RE
10:55–11:15	Task: Spelling/RE
11:15–11:35	Task: Perceptual motor skills/RE
11:35–12:30	Clean-up/Lunch
12:30–12:50	Task: Quiet rest/RE
12:50– 1:10	Task: Individual reading/RE
1:10– 1:30	Task: Fine motor skills (varied: pegboards, puzzles, etc.)/RE
1:30– 1:50	Task: Group activity/RE
1:50– 2:00	Task: Clean-up/Dismissal

This sample schedule was adapted from one developed by Mrs. Jackie Damaske.

---

*The initial task or tasks would involve listening to you point out how the room is arranged, location and availability of the RE materials and activities, and possibly a tour of the room. It is a good idea to plan a class discussion task for the end of each day to evaluate the day's activities and work out problems. This time is for the *students* to share their feelings.

Activity II

For the students you worked with in Activity I, prepare a schedule for the entire *first day** of your Contingency Management program. Be sure that the timing adjusts to your recesses and lunch breaks. The tasks need not be stated in detail for each cycle. Do designate recess and lunch. Think in terms of twenty-minute cycles. The portion of each cycle which is left after a student has completed his task is his RE time. Try to design the individual student's task so that there are about ten minutes left at the end of each cycle for his RE time.

Cycle Time	Length (min.)	Task (exact definition optional, except for recesses, lunch)	Estimated Task Length (min.)
	20		10
	20		10
	20		10

We have emphasized that the Contingency Management system be used throughout the school day; however, if you are a secondary level teacher, a resource teacher, an education student, or in any other situation where you work with one group of students for only a *portion* of the day, you can effectively employ Contingency Management. The schedule for your students would still involve breaking the subject matter, or series of tasks, into twenty- to thirty-minute work and RE cycles. Below

*If you are a student teacher, or a teacher who works with a group of children for only part of a day, plan a shorter schedule using this format.

is an example of a schedule for a secondary level French class. Other adaptations appropriate for older students are described in chapter 6.

Cycle Time	Length (min.)	Task	Estimated Task Length (min.)
9:00–9:20	20	Vocabulary Review (student pairs) Self-Checklist/RE	10
9:20–9:50	30	Future Tense and Examples (Listening Task and Practice Exercise)/RE	20

TASKS FOR STUDENTS

Initially, all students will be doing the same or similar tasks at the same time; therefore, it is recommended that the tasks presented be slightly below grade or competency level. This insures that all students in the class will experience success when the program begins.

In chapter 6 you will find some suggestions for individualizing instruction once the system is established. Teaching the students how to function within the terms of the program is the first objective when the program begins. It is unlikely that *exactly* the same tasks will be appropriate for all the students in any one particular class. Some individualization is necessary from the very beginning or you will run the risk of building up resentments on the part of the slower students and/or boring other students with tasks that are too easy. Providing "mini" tasks for individuals is a simple way to meet students' needs. Instead of presenting a student with a full page of math problems which would be impossible for him to complete, cut the page in half. The method of requiring the student to complete several short pages of problems rather than one long page in one task period has been found successful by many teachers. When spot checking students' work, drawing a "happy face," marking "good" or "OK" on the paper leaves the student with a feeling of accomplishment. More difficult tasks should be introduced only after the program is well established; even then they should be brought in very gradually. Do everything you can to ensure that each student experiences success in the early days of the program. Provide students with answer sheets so that they may check and correct their own work if they are able.

Clear directions and well-organized tasks are essential to student success. Watch your students as they work. Quickly help the one who is confused or gets slowed down. Change or shorten the task assignment if necessary; be willing to accept approximation of desired performance. Tasks which are too difficult only frustrate the student and inhibit learning.

Group work and discussions may be handled just like any other type of task. The students receive RE time for sitting quietly, responding when called upon, waiting their turn, and answering questions correctly.

It is still possible to conduct reading groups, math groups, and enrichment or remedial programs under this system. While the teacher conducts the reading group, the other students are doing tasks at their desks. Students in the Bluebird Reading Group are simply scheduled to meet with the teacher at 10:00 A.M., for example, and Johnny can be scheduled to read about Einstein's theory on pages 24–36 in his science book at 11:00 A.M.

If you are a teacher, go now to Activity III;
If you are an education student, turn to Activity IV.

Activity III

Now, describe exactly the tasks you will present to your students (the same students you worked with in Activity I) when you begin the Contingency Management program. It is a good idea to prepare *more* tasks than you think you will actually need. Experienced teachers say to plan at least three times as many tasks as you *think* you will need! Remember, the tasks should be short and simple — and ones which all students can complete with a high degree of success in about ten minutes.

Detailed List of Tasks

Example: Individual Reading — read pages 14 and 15 in Blue Book. Answer the questions on worksheet.

1.

2.

3.

4.

5.

6.

7.

8.

9.

10.

11.

12.

13.

14.

15.

16.

17.

18.

19.

20.

Now turn to Activity V.

Activity IV

For the students you worked with in Activity I, plan and develop a list of tasks at their level which you and their classroom teacher decide upon. List your ideas below.

Detailed List of Tasks

Example: 10 two-place addition problems

1.

2.

3.

4.

5.

6.

7.

8.

9.

10.

Now turn to Activity V.

Activity V

When you have carefully planned the tasks you will be presenting to your students, actually begin to collect and construct the worksheets and materials which will be used. Don't hesitate to tear appropriate individual pages out of workbooks the students are using, or to cut a page in half.

Then make a work folder for each student. In each folder place a copy of the first day's schedule and *all* the assigned task materials, worksheets, and directions.

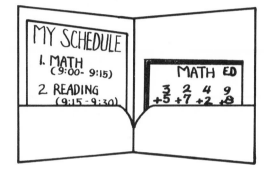

EXPLAINING THE SYSTEM TO THE STUDENTS*

Step five in planning a Contingency Management program is explaining to the students how the system will work. This is best handled through a group discussion.

To prepare for this discussion, make a chart or overhead transparency similar to the one shown on page 63. The visual should illustrate how the program will work; that is, how each day will be divided up into times for tasks and times for rewarding and fun activities. All the procedures for explaining the system to the class are presented in frames 15–23, filmstrip 4; review these frames now.

Review with the students the RE menu you previously planned together (Activity I). Add to the menu any new suggestions from the students; decide where the RE activities and materials will be located in the room.

During the discussion with your students remember to:

a. explain that they will be responsible for completing a specific amount of work;

b. tell them that *as soon as* their work is finished, they will have a few minutes of free time to do something listed on the RE menu;

c. agree upon the *rules* for signalling your attention (to help with task or to check completed assignment);

d. select a *signal* to be used to call the students back from RE time to the task area;

e. establish the rules for moving appropriately from one area of the classroom to another;

f. reassure your students that this system is as new to you as it is to them and that problems will arise but will be worked out cooperatively. Be honest.

---

*Plan to read the first section of chapter 5 before you present the Contingency Management program to your students.

OUR NEW PROGRAM

DO SOME WORK....

HAVE SOME FREE TIME....

DO SOME MORE WORK...

HAVE SOME MORE FREE TIME...

WORK....

FREE TIME....

WORK IS WHATEVER IS ASSIGNED,

FREE TIME IS WHATEVER YOU WANT TO DO!

IF

1. YOUR WORK IS FINISHED CORRECTLY.

2. YOU RESPECT THE RIGHT OF OTHERS.

3. YOU REMEMBER SAFETY RULES.

4. YOU REMEMBER SCHOOL RULES.

Task IX

*Self-Test on Planning a Contingency
Management Program in the Classroom—II*

> *Directions:* In the following questions, mark *all* the alternatives which you think are correct.

1. The first two steps in planning a Contingency Management program are making a menu and arranging the classroom.

   The third step is: _____

   _____

2. How and when (i.e., under what conditions) will you dismiss your students to the RE area?

   _____

   _____

   _____

3. The fourth step in planning a Contingency Management program is to design and collect tasks for each cycle. In the *beginning*, tasks should be:
   a. individualized
   b. short and simple
   c. similar for all students
   d. challenging

4. The final step is explaining the Contingency Management system to your students; list the things you would tell them about how the program will work:

   _____

   _____

   _____

Check your answers with those on the following page.

Answer Sheet—Task IX

1. developing a schedule

2. when task has been completed successfully or student has made an acceptable attempt; and when student's work has been checked off

3. b. short and simple
   c. similar for all students

4. they are responsible for completing some work
   when work is finished they will have free time
   must return to task area upon signal
   teacher will check work and excuse students to RE area
   etc., etc.

5

Implementing a
Contingency
Management Program

SETTING THE STAGE FOR IMPLEMENTING

Now that you have learned all the steps in a Contingency Management system and have created an RE menu, planned a schedule, and designed tasks for your students, you are ready to implement your new program. If you are a student teacher, discuss your plan with your supervising teacher.

SUN	MON	TUE	WED	THU	FRI	SAT
			1	2	3	4
5	6	7	8	9	10	11
12	13	14	15	16	17	18

The remainder of this chapter is organized into five sections which correspond to the first five days that you implement with your students. *These are five successive days.* If you are a teacher you must conduct the Contingency Management program *every day* for it to be successful. In other words, don't begin the system unless you are prepared to use it consistently. If you are a resource teacher or education student and do not see the same students every day, you must plan to use Contingency Management *every time* you see them. The students must learn that this is the way their time with *you* is structured regardless of what happens on intervening days.

If possible, your new program should begin on a Monday. On the preceding school day (Friday), you need to accomplish two things:

1. *Explain and discuss the new system* with your students. (Refer to chapter 4 for ideas.)

   At this time, you may want to have the students make their own *desk signals.*

   It is also necessary to refer to your list of materials and equipment for REs (Activity I — Part B) and remind the students to bring in the materials they wish to donate to the RE area.

2. *Rearrange your classroom.* After the students have left for the day, set up the task and RE areas. Refer to your planned room arrangement and HPB list (Task VII and Activity I — Part B).

   Be certain that all the needed materials and equipment are ready for use as REs.

To insure that your Contingency Management program is a successful one, take a few minutes to review the steps listed below:

FIRST DAY CHECKLIST   √

> 1. The menu that you and your students have made is posted in your classroom (Chapter 3, pages 27–28).

FIRST DAY CHECKLIST (Continued)

2. The activities and necessary materials are ready in the RE area (Chapter 3, pages 33–34).

3. A schedule is made for the first day (Chapter 4, pages 53–54).

4. A folder is ready for each student and contains tasks for the first day (Chapter 4, page 61).

5. Extra tasks are prepared (three times as many tasks as you think you'll need) (Chapter 4, pages 56–57).

6. The students know about the program and how it will work (Chapter 4, page 62).

7. Desk signals are ready for each student (Chapter 4, pages 51–52).

8. You and your students have agreed upon a non-verbal signal to signify the end of RE time (Chapter 4, page 52).

This program has been designed to provide careful guidelines for planning a Contingency Management program. If you have completed all the steps sequentially, the chances of your program being a success are excellent. However, when we set out to develop new behavior patterns, it is almost inevitable that things will not proceed exactly as planned. Unexpected situations are almost certain to arise. For these reasons, the following exercise, which is based on classroom experiences of teachers who became successful Contingency Managers,* is included.

---

*Special thanks to Dorothy Mortimer, James Shaw, Gerald Olson, Washington Elementary Schools, Phoenix, Arizona.

Task X

Directions: Assume the role of Contingency Manager. React to each situation described below. After choosing your solution, read the discussion following.

1. During an RE cycle, Bob and Beverly start yelling, each claiming the other had been using the cassette player. Beverly hits Bob. WHAT DO YOU DO?
   a. put the cassette player away and tell Bob and Beverly to select other RE activities
   b. send Beverly to the principal's office
   c. try to find out who is right
   d. remove both students from RE area, so that they are not permitted to participate in that RE cycle

2. Joy was given a task well within her ability. All the other students have completed their tasks and are in RE. Joy is just staring out the window. WHAT DO YOU DO?
   a. make a blindfold for Joy
   b. ignore her
   c. remind Joy that she must attempt her task before she gets any RE time
   d. tell Joy to get down to work

3. Ronny refuses to go to RE after task completion, saying that the activities in RE are for babies. WHAT DO YOU DO?
   a. remind Ronny that he had his chance to suggest activities for the RE menu
   b. ignore him
   c. find out what he would like to do; add this to the RE selection

4. When the signal to return to the task area is given, four students rush rapidly back, knocking desks and shelves all over the place. WHAT DO YOU DO?
   a. immediately excuse the rest of the class to another RE time for returning appropriately
   b. give these students twice as many tasks this time
   c. take their next RE time away from them

5. At each RE time Toby goes over to a corner and tugs at his hair. WHAT DO YOU DO?
   a. tell him to look at the menu and choose something
   b. leave him alone
   c. send Toby back to the task area

Check your answers with those on the following page.

Answer Sheet — Task X

1. Solution: Answer d., loss of privilege is the most appropriate response. Actually, this situation might indicate a need for some type of system whereby students can make reservations to use specific materials and equipment at a given time.

2. Solution: Answers b. and c. are both possible ways of dealing with the problem. At first, it would be preferable to ignore her and see if the problem eventually takes care of itself — chances are that Joy will not choose to spend the whole day looking out the window. If reminding her how the program works is not effective, the next step is to discuss the situation with the student. Ask the student if there is an RE she would like added to the menu. If necessary, "staring out the window" can be made contingent on task completion.

3. Solution: Answer c. should have been your choice. Remember that your goal at first is for the students to enjoy the program. If Ronny asks for an activity that is not immediately available, suggest that it be arranged for the next day, and that for today he should try some of the available REs. Simply ignoring this student would not be helpful because he might drop out of the program for the day.

4. Solution: Answer a. is the most effective approach because *appropriate* behavior is rewarded immediately in front of the disruptive students who are required to "wait out" that RE period. To give extra tasks to the disruptive students or to deny them their next RE would be a punishment (review comments on punishment in filmstrip 1 and also in chapter 1).

5. Solution: Answer b. is correct. Obviously, tugging at his hair is a high probability behavior for Toby, and as long as he is not disrupting others, or hurting himself, initially he should be allowed to engage in this behavior during RE time. If the behavior continues over several days, you might try the approach suggested in answer a.; another alternative would be to ask Toby what he would prefer to do.

PROGRAM DAY 1

On this day you begin your planned schedule with your students. Students will arrive to find the classroom set up, ready to go. Students take their places, where they find their folders and desk signals and begin their first week. For every day of the first week, additional hints and ideas are provided. We suggest that you read the following section after your first program day.

Now BEGIN THE PROGRAM WITH YOUR STUDENTS!!!

You did it!! Congratulations, we hope that you and your students are excited about the new program. To insure that the program continues to run smoothly, here are some points to consider for tomorrow.*

Task Area

Insist that the students exhibit appropriate behavior in the task area at all times. If a student talks out of turn, merely *ignore* him until he is quiet. The moment the student becomes quiet, go quickly to his side, praise him or answer his question. Stick to your nonverbal desk signals. Avoid verbal commands such as "get down to work," "raise your hand," etc. Remember, it is only necessary to *spot-check* papers.

Returning to Task Area

Emphasis should be on immediate return to task area. Reinforce prompt returning to the task area by noticeably attending to the students who return first. A surprise reinforcement every so often to individuals or the whole group for prompt return to the task area will tend to keep this behavior alive.

RE Time

Only hazardous things should be put up and machinery turned off. Students return at next RE time to continue with or replace items in proper places.

Plan with children and work out the responsibility of major clean-up times.

Don't let an obsessive desire for neatness be a deterrent to a successful, interesting, exciting RE area.

Be prepared for initial clustering and confusion; this begins to taper off quickly; encourage children to work out sharing systems and group cooperation; mediate problems on the spot.

Children are to be responsible and not wasteful in the use of materials; they must learn how to operate equipment and when

---

*Contributed by Jackie Damaske, Contingency Manager; adapted from Volkmor, Langstaff, and Higgins, *Structuring the Classroom for Success*, 1974.

to seek help; carelessness is discouraged immediately and loss of privilege results if necessary.

The child who cannot decide on an RE activity may simply need help in making choices. Narrow the range of choices for this child by offering him two activities at a time instead of the entire menu.

Remember, during the first week or so, students are excused to the RE area from the task area *individually*, but return from RE to the task area as a *group.*

If a student continually lags behind after RE time:

> Keep his work from him for the amount of time he lags. This means that his next RE time will be shorter.

> Reinforce appropriate returning to task area with all students more frequently by immediately excusing them to another RE time.

Be sure to explain consequences of inappropriate responses and behavior to all the students in the class so everyone knows what is expected. Be sure to do this at the very beginning of the program *before* any problems arise.

Suggestions for Preventing Undesirable Behavior

Numbers one and two are *musts.* However, if they do not work, try number three, etc.

1. Undesirable behavior is ignored as much as possible.
2. Desirable behavior is reinforced as much as possible.
3. Desired behavior exhibited by other students is reinforced within earshot and eyeshot of misbehaving student.
4. Student is reminded of basic rules of others' rights and consequences in a discussion with him individually.
5. Student may not participate in *any* activities.
   a. Work is removed and all items he seeks to work with.
   b. Decision for returning to work is left up to him within specific time limits.

Last Resort

6. Student is removed to another part of the room within sight of teacher, but isolated from others.

Whenever a confrontation is necessary, plan a time to sit and discuss it with the student when you are both more objective, so that you can renew your relationship and alleviate resentments.

If you are at Step 4 and haven't given Steps 1, 2 and 3 a good try, you are cheating yourself *and* the student. (Volkmor, Langstaff, Higgins 1974, pp. 116–17)

PROGRAM DAY 2

Gather new tasks for student folders, but basically repeat schedule used on Program Day 1.

The Contingency Manager's role, as described by Venita Dee of Scottsdale, Arizona:

Probably the most important thing to operating a successful C. M. program is the willingness of the person involved to do a lot of things: be extremely consistent, be willing and able to change when the students' needs are no longer the same, be willing to accept approximations of the desired behavior, be willing to look for positive ways of rewarding a student, be willing to be inventive. We have been moved around a lot and have had to share our room with others . . . so I have found it is not so much the way the room is arranged as what the teacher expects within what she has to work with. I have found that it is important to keep the room as simple as possible so that when I do put something up, it is meaningful and so regarded by the kids. I spell out a lot of things, in writing for the kids, so that there is no chance of misunderstanding . . . these things are blunt, simple, direct, but always understood.

In my class I don't have a long time to have each child . . . the longest is somewhere around several weeks, so what we have to do must be easily understood and quickly grasped, hence the need for directness. This is the nice part about the program: there is *always* a choice for the child and I am always there to follow through with whatever has been set up . . . and NO ONE either gets the chance or has the opportunity to NAG!!! (Even though the kids, I have found, have a great problem at first understanding this . . . they expect teacher to nag!!! . . . what does this say about us??)

Handling Problems in the RE Area and Some More RE Ideas!

The following was contributed by Gwen Baldwin, a Contingency Manager from Las Vegas:

My biggest problem in the initial phases, which is hardly worth mentioning, was dealing with arguing and fighting in the RE area. It seemed everyone wanted to use the same thing at the same time. I solved this problem by making tagboard tags for the items in question. They could play with these items only when they had the proper tag around their neck.

As for RE ideas, I find at the beginning of the year they mostly play with toys. However, that gradually dies out and they turn to other things. Probably the most unusual is this: There is a long row of bushes next to a fence, near our room. The boys call it their fort and they sit in behind them and talk. . . .

Another RE idea that is popular and also helpful is that they like to help others with their work.

These are some ideas from Eloise E. Daniels of Escondido, California:

Braids of rug yarn about 3 feet long worn across the shoulders show that child in RE area is official.

Label names of tagboard, about 2x8 inches, placed in the space left by the game (or other choice in RE area) enables easy return, keeping shelves neat.

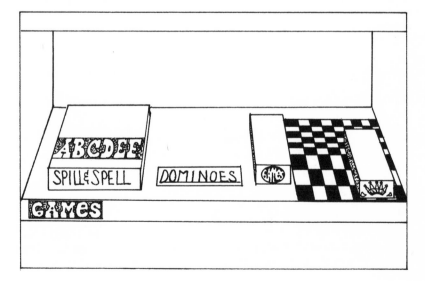

When introducing a new RE game, make "learning how to play the game" a *task* for one small group at a time. Actually sit down and teach the group the rules for playing the game during one task time. This will serve to head off problems that might arise in RE area because students don't understand the directions.

PROGRAM DAY 3

Gather new tasks, but basically repeat the schedule used on Program Day 1.

For Individual Reading I have worked out a system that works for me. Students read in their own individual books (Sullivan Series), write new words (in notebook). When finished, they are excused to RE Area, then called out individually to read to me and Instructional Aide. There are extra ditto and work sheets in RE Area. I will also call them up for other periods of work when there is free time. *(Beverly J. Scarla*, Glendale, Arizona)

More RE Ideas

RE Menu specials include:

1. Working in cafeteria
2. Working in library
3. Working with P.E. Instructor with kindergarten children
4. Saving RE for weekly party
5. Saving RE for walking field trip
6. Speech teacher had to use RE because students did not want to go to speech — students took an RE card to speech; if they performed, she punched card and they got extra RE. This worked out quite well.
7. To encourage some home work projects, students turn in workbooks; if correct and have done the assignments, they get 10 minutes extra RE.
8. Students allowed to get drinks and use restrooms without asking during their RE time — eliminates asking my permission. Students now display self-controlled behavior, not teacher control. *(Beverly Scarla)*

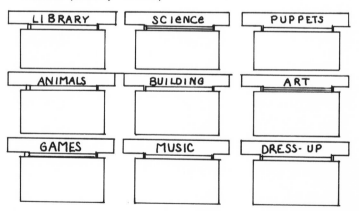

Perpetual Menu Board — Use pegboard, about 2 feet square, and fasten tagboard rows of pockets using brass paper fasteners. Cut "squatty T-shaped inserts" having names of menu choices. The menu is easily changed by having extra inserts made up. (*Eloise Daniels*)

If there are non-readers using the menu, make sketches instead of writing the items for the perpetual menu . . . later use the word in the same area.

We like the freshness which the children show after an RE break. They happily start to work on tasks to earn free time again. (*Eloise Daniels*)

Our RE Area has extra "Learning Centers" in it now. For example — Science Corner — with microscope, rocks, bugs, shells, etc.

Listening Center — with earphones so some can study Spanish — this became an RE.

Typing became an RE. I borrow a typewriter once a week — they go wild for this RE! (*Beverly Scarla*)

We also provide lots of new, interesting and challenging books, materials and even math assignments in the activity or reinforcement area. Many of our students become so successful academically that they would prefer to do academic tasks as reinforcers. We allow them to do this if they so choose. We also often encourage our students to be teacher aides during reinforcement time or to clean the room or to wash up the sink. We let the students, as a reward, correct the papers of the other students.

The variety of RE activities is only limited by the imagination of you and your students. (*Harry Rosenberg*, Visalia, California, talk presented at Special Study Institute, State of California, 1969.)

PROGRAM DAY 4

Gather new tasks, but basically repeat the schedule used on Program Day 1.

Changing the Contract

Throughout this program it has been emphasized that the contingency contract should, at first, require a rather small amount of work before the RE is given to the student. The length, amount, or quality of task behavior should be increased gradually. The amount, type, and frequency of the RE can also be changed as students progress. The contract should always be worded in such a way, however, that it is clear to the student that it is his performance or accomplishment that is being rewarded.

Even the most carefully planned student-teacher contract may occasionally fail; sometimes a verbal reaffirmation of the contract will help. If the student still does not, or cannot, perform, the teacher should immediately redesign or change the task. If this does not solve the problem, you should next consider the RE side of the contract. Perhaps the activities listed on the menu are no longer motivating, and it is time to plan a new RE menu with the students. Remember — when in doubt, ask the student! The responsibility of fulfilling the contract is shared by the teacher *and* the student.

PROGRAM DAY 5

Gather new tasks, but basically repeat the schedule used on Program Day 1.

Here are some additional thoughts and comments from teachers who are using Contingency Management:

I can't brag enough about the 100% effectiveness of the C.M. program. The class appears almost to run itself. I can honestly say that discipline problems do not exist!

A letter to the substitute teacher is in a plastic folder taped on my desk. The System is explained in simplicity. I have never encountered any problems. (*Beverly Scarla*)

Of course, I am still using a C.M. Program and probably always will. The two most outstanding reasons are (1) my physical and mental state and (2) the (almost) elimination of behavior problems.

Before C.M., I was mentally and physically exhausted at the end of the day. I felt mean and I took it out on the children and my family. Since C.M., I am just as cheerful at the end of the day as I was at the beginning and I have enough energy to continue my other chores.

My behavior problems are nearly eliminated because I treat my students like responsible individuals. They have the freedom of choosing how they will behave and perform their duties, which gives them the feeling they are in control. Of course, because I ignore the unwanted behavior and because of the RE, they almost always make the right choice. (*Gwen Baldwin*)

Implementation of C.M. in my classroom has helped me to be a more organized and efficient "director" of learning, while my students have assumed more and more responsibility for their own acquisition of knowledge.

We used the C.M. model in a summer school program involving 20 hyperactive, learning disabled children. Many of these students had previous records of disruptive classroom behavior. Results of this program confirmed the effectiveness of Contingency Management in controlling undesired behavior and in promoting learning. In some cases the structured C.M. Program allowed children to function well in the classroom without the use of medication. (*Ruth Kass*, Scottsdale, Arizona)

Feedback from other successful Contingency Managers has indicated that informing or even involving parents significantly adds to the success of the program. Parents may request help in applying Contingency Management principles at home with their children.

Task XI

You have now implemented the Contingency Management program in your classroom for one week. Congratulations! The next step is to begin planning for next week — to provide for a bit more individualization of tasks, and to make a few adjustments and refinements. Before you begin this, take a few moments to consider the following situations (did it happen to you?) and possible solutions (how do you handle the problem?).

1. Carl complains to the teacher that he hasn't been able to use the chessboard as it was tied up by Joe and Jim. WHAT DO YOU DO?

_____

_____

_____

2. Mary complains that she just wants to read her reading book at her task desk rather than go to RE. WHAT DO YOU DO?

_____

_____

_____

3. The whole class comes back from lunch and all but five students are whooping it up and fooling around. Five students have their signals on "WORKING" and are at their assigned tasks. WHAT DO YOU DO?

_____

_____

_____

4. Mike has not earned RE time after math task every day this week. He has completed three-fourths of the sheet correctly when RE time was finished for the rest of the group. WHAT DO YOU DO?

_____

_____

_____

5. Richie has not done any arithmetic all week — has missed RE each time — sits at his desk and sulks. Each day you have shortened the assignment and adjusted the difficulty level. WHAT DO YOU DO?

_____

_____

_____

6. Barry has been completing every task correctly in three minutes and is having twice as much RE time as any other classmate. WHAT DO YOU DO?

_____

_____

_____

7. Students are all completing their individual tasks at their competency levels close to the allotted task times, and in RE are engaged in their "things." WHAT DO YOU DO?

_____

_____

_____

Check your responses with the solutions on the following page.

Answer Sheet — Task XI

It Could Happen to You . . .

Possible Solutions:

1. Ask the kids for solutions.

   Set up a reservation system for the chess set and other very popular REs.

   Get another chess set.

   Establish rule that game must not extend beyond 2 or 3 RE times.

2. Let her do it!! Reading is an RE for Mary.

3. Immediately excuse the five working students to RE. Reinforce "coming into room behavior" (as a task) every time for a few days by excusing students who behaved appropriately to RE.

4. Ask Mike!

   Modify the *amount* of task required from Mike — it may be too long.

   Remember, REWARD APPROXIMATIONS — it says he did three-fourths of the sheet *correctly* — the problem is probably related to amount of work required.

5. Ask Richie! — discuss the problem with him.

   REs may not have a great enough appeal to him — seek out his HPB — there's got to be one somewhere!

6. May be time to modify Barry's contract — length and amount of task may be increased; give him two tasks to do; discuss this with him.

7. What?? Big deal, you've got it made!!!

6

Maintaining and Adapting the System

PLANNING FOR THE SECOND WEEK: KEEPING THE SYSTEM GOING

Now it is time to prepare your schedule and tasks for the *second* week of implementation. Keep these things in mind:

Take your cues from the students. If they seem to have a *good grasp* on how the system itself works, you might begin to individualize their tasks a bit; if not, continue to emphasize the

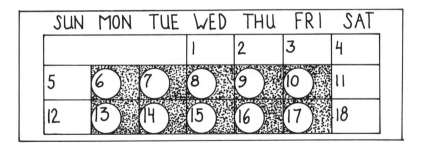

process and concentrate on making directions clear and self-explanatory *and* work on any problem areas.

Make changes toward individualization gradually.

Revise the menu; ask the kids how RE is going. Be ready to add or delete activities available for free time according to the children's interests. Keep the menu flexible.

Talk the system over with the kids. How is it going? What things do they like and what things don't they like?

Continually monitor the *amount* of RE time kids are having; if it is *under* ten minutes for most of them, the tasks are probably too difficult or long; if it is *over* ten minutes for most of the class, then it is probably time to increase the amount or difficulty of tasks.

THE SCHEDULE

After the basic Contingency Management system is thoroughly familiar to both the students and teacher, the schedule should be adjusted to allow for greater individualization.

This is a sample schedule* to be used when you are ready to individualize. Notice that the cycles are now *thirty minutes* in length. The task time is twenty minutes (longer tasks or combinations of tasks) and the RE time remains at ten minutes.

TIME	ACTIVITY
9:00– 9:30	Task: Meeting & Gross motor Activity/RE
9:30–10:00	Task: Reading & Writing practice/RE
10:00–10:30	Task: Math/RE
10:30–10:50	Task: Recess/RE

*This sample schedule is adapted from one developed by Mrs. Jackie Damaske.

TIME	ACTIVITY
10:50–11:20	Task: Spelling and Phonics/RE
11:20–12:30	Clean-up/Lunch
12:30– 1:00	Task: Rest & Listening activity/RE
1:00– 1:30	Task: Individual reading & Fine motor skills/RE
1:30– 1:50	Task: Group activity (discussion and evaluation of the day & planning for tomorrow/RE
1:50– 2:00	Clean-up/Dismissal

Task XII

Prepare a schedule for the second week of the Contingency Management program in your classroom. Think in terms of longer cycles (perhaps thirty minutes each).

Cycle Time	Length (min.)	Task

Extra Schedule Work Form

This schedule plan sheet can be completed after you have implemented for at least two weeks. Continue to use TASK/RE cycles.

Cycle Time	Length (min.)	Task

THE TASKS

Tasks may be combined so that easier ones are coupled with more complicated ones — but tasks must still be reasonable and attainable. Some longer tasks can be scheduled to extend through two or three task times with REs in between.

Begin to program in some small group work as tasks; designate a group discussion table and schedule various small groups there at task times throughout the day.

Now gather and construct your tasks for the first day of your *second* week of implementation.

SOME VARIATIONS FOR LATER ON

1. *A Super Schedule.* Contingency Management can be successfully integrated with almost any system of classroom
organization already set up.

A sample schedule developed for using Contingency Management in a classroom organized around Learning Centers
is shown on pages 96–98. This schedule evolved to this point
very gradually. The classroom at the beginning of the year
was divided into a TASK and RE area. Activity Centers were
set up, one or two at a time, until there were six centers
plus RE areas and the entire class was accommodated at
the same time in the centers.

There are five to six students in each group (about thirty
students total). Two groups of similar ability level are combined to form a reading or math group of about ten students.

Reading and math groups may work intensively with the
teacher during the times allotted. At other times, the teacher
rotates from center to center.

Special cycles are set aside for teaching new concepts to
a large group or the entire class. Social studies, language
arts, map or dictionary skills are a few of the academic areas
which may be handled in the "Input Time." Social studies
could also be covered in the A-V Center.

The activity centers contain preprepared Activity or Task
Cards, follow-up sheets, experiments and/or other assignments which can be accomplished in about a twenty-minute
period. Students may each have a Master Schedule which
specifies the task to be done at each center.

Students participate in REs in other sections of the room
or quietly at a particular center of their choosing, if there
is room.

SUPER DELUXE SCHEDULE

8:30– 8:45	Start the Day: pledge, etc.
8:45– 8:50	RE
8:50– 9:10	Group 1 — Science Center Group 2 — Listening/Viewing Center Group 3 — Language Center (Spelling, etc.) Group 4 — Games Center (Reading, Phonics, etc.) Group 5 ⎫ — Reading Center ⎱ Reading Group Group 6 ⎭ — Reading Center ⎰ with teacher
9:10– 9:15	RE
9:15– 9:30	Recess
9:30– 9:50	Group 1 ⎫ — Group 2 ⎭ — Reading Center Group 3 — Science Center Group 4 — Listening/Viewing Center Group 5 — Language Center Group 6 — Games Center
9:50–10:00	RE
10:00–10:20	Group 1 — Listening/Viewing Center Group 2 — Science Center Group 3 ⎫ — Group 4 ⎭ — Reading Center Group 5 — Games Center Group 6 — Language Center
10:20–10:25	RE
10:25–10:45	Group 1 ⎫ — Group 2 ⎭ — Math Center Group 3 — Games Center Group 4 — Language Center Group 5 — Listening/Viewing Center Group 6 — Science Center

SUPER DELUXE SCHEDULE (Continued)

10:45–10:55	RE
10:55–11:15	Group 1 — Language Center Group 2 — Games Center Group 3 ⎫ Group 4 ⎭ — Math Center Group 5 — Science Center Group 6 — Listening/Viewing Center
11:15–11:20	RE
11:20–11:45	Group 1 — Games Center Group 2 — Language Center Group 3 — Listening/Viewing Center Group 4 — Science Center Group 5 ⎫ Group 6 ⎭ — Math Center
11:45–11:50	RE
11:50–12:00	Clean up — Ready for lunch
12:00–12:40	Lunch
12:40–12:45	RE
12:45– 1:05	Input time for new concepts — Teacher directed
1:05– 1:10	RE
1:10– 1:30	Input time for new concepts — Teacher directed
1:30– 1:35	RE
1:35– 1:55	P.E.
1:55– 2:00	RE

SUPER DELUXE SCHEDULE (Continued)

2:00– 2:20	Choose a task at a Center or sharing
2:20– 2:25	RE
2:25– 2:45	Class Meeting — How did the day go?
2:45– 3:00	Clean-up task/RE areas
3:00	Dismiss

2. *Daily Contracting with Individual Students.* Once the system has been established with the group, different time schedules can be worked out with individual students as they become ready; let the student become involved in selecting and setting his or her own work goals.

Daily contracts may be set up between you and the student, when he is ready to choose the work he needs and is able to be responsible on his own for completing it.

Hankins, in discussing a report by Black (1969), gives a good description of this type of contingency:

In the beginning, students contracted each morning for a day's work. The contract included a list of assignments in subject-matter areas. The subject areas, materials to be used, page numbers, and any specific directions felt necessary were written on a transparency, put on an overhead projector, and projected on a screen for approximately one-half hour each morning. (p. 299)

This approach obviously permits students to progress at their own rates; they can complete the assignments in their order of choosing.

Children enjoy some way of checking themselves off; it gives them an extra sense of accomplishment. Credit cards for work completed may be devised for this purpose. This gives the child a deeper feeling of commitment and responsibility. A certain amount of time may be prescribed until he earns a day off or some other congratulatory sign. Some teachers have successfully used student recorders for checking off each other's work and excusing each other to the RE area.

CHECK CARD	MON	TUE	WED	THU	BILL FRI
READING	✓		✓		✓
MATH		✓	✓		
SPELLING	✓			✓	

3. *Longer Term Contracts.* Weekly contracts can also be set up. A dittoed weekly schedule, Monday through Friday, with time cycles for each day can be passed out to students at a Monday morning "class meeting." The task that morning is for each student to contract for a specific amount of work in each subject area to be completed by Friday. He fills in his weekly schedule, it is approved by or negotiated with the teacher, and he is on his own. He can complete his tasks in any order, schedule his own task completion/reward cycles, and check in with teacher at various points along the way.

Another adaptation related to setting up longer term contracts involves the concept of accumulating free time over a period of days. Williams and Anandam (1973) state:

Presumably a student could earn an average of fifteen minutes free time each day, and save his free time until Friday, when he would have an hour's free time. If this were a junior or senior high school, the student might simply take the period off on Friday. A major advantage of having free time each day, as opposed to accumulating large blocks of free time, is the immediacy of reinforcement for appropriate behavior. Yet, you may find that some of your students are able to delay gratification for extended periods and are more productive when allowed to accumulate free time. (p. 67)

SELF-CONTRACTING

At the high school and college levels, contracting for grades can be used successfully. The instructor and students work together to determine various options for assignments and the number and quality of those assignments required to earn various letter grades for the course. The final version of the contract is given in written form to each class member. Within a week, each student must submit his or her contract including the grade and the specific assignments he or she would complete to earn the grade.

The contract greatly simplifies the grading process. At the end of the prescribed period, the conditions of the contract either *have* or *have not* been met. Students who do not fulfill their contracted commitments can really blame no one but themselves since they selected their goals. (Hankins 1973, p. 295)

Self-contracting may also be utilized at the elementary and junior high levels. Following is an example of a contract form which can be used for self-contracting with younger students. The teacher moves slowly from maintaining major control for task decisions to allowing the student more and more freedom in determining his own curriculum and how he will learn it. In student controlled contracts:

... the student has the major responsibility for designing the problem, asking the questions and evaluating his answers. ... With both command and responsibility for the learning process, it will normally take longer for the student to organize learning activities which seem scattered or haphazard, into what the student deems to be orderly and reasonable for him. Once this plateau is reached creativity may begin. (Glavin 1974, p. 87)

STUDENT-TEACHER CONTRACT

Contract Terms:

Performance Objectives:

STUDENT-TEACHER CONTRACT (Continued)

RE:

The student,_____(name)_____, upon finishing the performance objective, will spend_____minutes in the RE area. He
or she will be free to choose those activities which he or she
enjoys.

Contract Length_____ to _____

Subject Area or
Behavior Area_____

Teacher's Name _____

Student's Name _____

Glossary

Approximations: successful attempts to complete a task.

Contingency Management: a contract system in which the students' successful task completion is consistently rewarded by free time activity. Receiving a reward is made contingent on task completion.

Contingency Manager: a teacher, parent, or any individual who uses a contingency system in managing the behavior of others.

Contract: an agreement (written or verbal) between teacher and student stating a specific task or amount of work to be done and the reward available upon completion of the work or task.

Cycle: a specific amount of classroom time (usually 20–30 minutes) during which students complete tasks and then engage in reward activities.

High Probability Behaviors (HPBs): behaviors which are enjoyed by the individual and which he frequently chooses to engage in when given the opportunity.

Low Probability Behaviors (LPBs): behaviors which occur infrequently and which the teacher would like to increase.

RE Area: a designated area in the classroom where all equipment and materials needed for REs are available.

RE Menu: a written list of activities from which students may choose during free time. The menu is generated by the students and the teacher together.

Reinforcing Event (RE): activities (HPBs) and materials which students *choose* and which are rewarding to *them.*

Schedule: a carefully planned, written outline of the daily program in the classroom. The schedule is made up of a continuous series of cycles and specifies a task for each cycle.

Signal: a nonverbal device (lights, bell) to notify students when it is time to return from the RE area to begin a new task.

Task: academic work or behavior (e.g., sitting in seat) which the teacher requires the student to complete (LPB).

Task Area: a designated area in the classroom where students complete academic tasks.

Bibliography

Addison, R. and Homme, L. "The Reinforcing Event (RE) Menu." *National Society for Programmed Instruction* 5 (1966): 8–9.

Berman, Mark L., ed. *Motivation and Learning: Applying Contingency Management Techniques.* Englewood Cliffs, N. J.: Educational Technology Publications, 1971.

Black, D. E. "A Contract Plan for Teaching Fifth Grade at Jefferson Elementary School in Kingsport, Tennessee." Master's Thesis, 1969.

Glavin, J. P. *Behavioral Strategies for Classroom Management.* Columbus, Ohio: Charles E. Merrill, 1974.

Hankins, N. E. *Psychology for Contemporary Education.* Columbus, Ohio: Charles E. Merrill, 1973.

Haring, N. G. and Phillips, E. L. *Analysis and Modification of Classroom Behavior.* Englewood Cliffs, N. J.: Prentice-Hall, 1972.

Homme, L.; Csanyi, A. P.; Gonzales, M. A.; and Rechs, J. R. *How to Use Contingency Contracting in the Classroom.* Champaign, Ill.: Research Press, 1970.

Homme, L. and Tosti, D. *Behavior Technology: Motivation and Contingency Management.* San Rafael, Ca.: Individual Learning Systems, 1971.

Sulzer, B. and Mayer, G. R. *Behavior Modification Procedures for School Personnel.* Hinsdale, Ill.: Dryden, 1972.

Volkmor, C. B.; Langstaff, A. L.; and Higgins, M. *Structuring the Classroom for Success.* Columbus, Ohio: Charles E. Merrill, 1974.

Williams, R. L. and Anandam, K. *Cooperative Classroom Management.* Columbus, Ohio: Charles E. Merrill, 1973.